Taylor Swift Trivia

Fun Facts, Quotes, Quizzes & More

Contents

FACT 1

1. She's a Self-Taught Musician
If there's one thing you should know about Taylor, it's that once she sets her mind on something, she's going to follow through. The talented singer proved this at the age of 12 when she learned how to play a 12-string guitar all by herself (well, with the little help of a repairman who taught her how to play three cords).

The rest was all down to her, though – she spent at least four hours a day practicing until she perfected her playing skills.

2. She Won a Talent Competition Aged 11
At the young age of 11, Taylor Swift won a local talent competition by covering the LeAnn Rimes song, Big Deal. Evidently, her love for LeAnn shines through her own similar music. Likewise, Taylor also writes deeply emotional songs that cover the ups and downs she's been through.

3. Taylor Grew Up on a Christmas Tree Farm
Is there anywhere cooler to grow up in other than a place that revolves around the most wonderful time of the year? It's true – Taylor Swift spent most of her childhood growing up on a Christmas tree farm until the age of 14. She even got stuck in and helped her dad by debugging the trees to make sure they didn't infest the house.

4. Taylor's a Real Estate Pro
Taylor knows how to invest her money wisely! With her hefty pay check, she's got onto the property ladder and invested her cash in not one, but eight properties, over four states, that are worth over $81 million. Her property empire includes an estate and a house

5. She Has Over 20 Songs Dedicated to Exes
This piece of trivia is no secret to music fans. The blonde beauty has penned over 20 songs about her ex-boyfriends. From Harry Styles to John Mayer and Jake Gyllenhaal, Taylor has covered many songs dedicated to her love, heartbreak and raw emotion.

One thing is for sure, the music mastermind has built an entire empire off the memories of her exes. These songs have helped her become the fourth most successful female singer of all time.

6. Taylor's Lucky Number is 13
Unlike others who hate the connotation of number 13, Swiftie believes that it's her lucky number, especially because it's her birthday (she was born on December 13th).

Her first album also went gold on the 13th week, she won an award when she sat in the 13th row, and her first number one hit had a 13-second intro. With all this being said, you can probably judge why the number 13 is so important to the megastar.

7. She Dreamed of Being a Broadway Star
Before Taylor even laid eyes on songwriting, she had her eyes set on the big stage. As she had acting and singing classes from a young age, she hoped to join both her passions and performing on-stage, but after endless rejections in the Big Apple, Taylor changed direction and started songwriting, instead.

8. She Also Wanted to be a Stockbroker

Before she fell in love with music, Taylor Swift wanted to become a stockbroker like her father. That said, when her family moved to Tennessee, she found her real passion – music.

9. Taylor Made Her Debut in 'CSI'

Taylor Swift is not only known for her killer vocals, stage presence and songwriting skills, but also for her on-screen performances. She first debuted as Haley Jones on CSI, before making a cameo appearance in Hannah Montana: The Movie. Since then, she's appeared in Valentine's Day, The Giver and Cats.

10. She's an 12-Time Grammy Award Winner

This cool fact about Taylor will make you proud of the Folklore star. At the mere age of just 34, this pop-icon has 12 Grammy awards tucked safely under her belt. In 2010 at just 20-years-old, Taylor made history when she became the youngest solo artist to win Album of the Year for Fearless (a feat now beaten by Billie Eilish).

Taylor has even bagged the Billboard award for 'Woman of the Year' not once, but twice (in 2011 and 2014). That's more times than any other female pop artist!

11. She Has a Framed Picture with Kanye

This Taylor Swift fact comes as a real surprise! Believe it or not, she has a framed photo of her famous feud with Kanye West, where he rudely interrupted her acceptance speech during the 2009 VMAs. The frame is placed underneath a handwritten note that says: "Life is full of interruptions".

12. She Was Once Against Streaming Sites

At a time when most artists embraced the arrival of streaming websites, Taylor refused to release her album, Red on the music-streaming site Spotify. She withheld all her songs and embarked on a three-year spat with the site over receiving low royalties on her songs.

After a while, Taylor gave in and made her entire library available on Spotify again. She claims this was due to her 1989 album passing 10 million in sales, but many speculate that it was because her rival Katy Perry was set to debut her new album on the service on the same day.

13. Taylor Won $1 Million in a Lawsuit

Taylor was reportedly groped during a meet-and-greet in Denver by Radio DJ, David Mueller. Although she aired the incident, she didn't demand a single dollar.

Instead, she wanted to make the assault public and prove herself a role model to other women. Following the report, the DJ then sued the Reputation singer for ruining his career (as if he didn't do that on his own!). She then counter-sued the DJ and won exactly $1 million in the lawsuit.

14. Her Household Interior is…Weird

Along with the framed picture of her run-in with Kanye West, T Swizzle also has a fish tank full of vintage baseballs. If that's not bonkers enough, she has a rail of white nightgowns that she throws on when her pal, Lena Dunham is visiting, to feel like they are "pioneer women".

15. She's Named After James Taylor
Here's a fun fact about Taylor's life you certainly didn't know. Her parents are huge fans of iconic singer James Taylor and they loved him so much that they wanted to name Swiftie after him. With the name came the same career path, and the pair even had the chance of performing together at a benefit in 2011.

16. Her Grandma was a Professional Opera Singer
It's no surprise that the vocal flair runs in Taylor's family – her grandma, Marjorie Moehlenkamp-Finlay was a professional opera singer and always influenced Taylor to sing and pursue a career in music.

17. Taylor's Never Been to Therapy
Instead of confiding in a trained professional, Taylor prefers to just discuss her feelings with her mom. Her mother has been with her through all of her ups and downs and is the only person that truly knows who she is and what she has been through. In 2019, Tay told Rolling Stone, "God, it takes so long to download somebody on the last 29 years of my life, and my mom has seen it all."

18. She's Super Charitable
While most celebs give back to their community to avoid hefty taxes, Taylor actually does it out of the goodness of her heart. She donated $15,500 to a fan whose mother had been in a coma for three years, without forgetting the $17,000 she gave to her home library, or the $10,000 she donated to a service dog of a boy with autism. These acts of kindness are just a few examples among the long list of good deeds Taylor has done since being in the limelight.

19. Taylor's a Self-Proclaimed Novelist
At an age (12) when most girls played with their hair and gossiped about their celeb crushes, Taylor was busy writing a novel. The non-autobiographical novel was titled A Girl Named Girl, and according to Tay's parents, they still have the copy! Who knows, it might be a best-seller if it ever gets released.

20. She's Scared of Being Tatted
An interesting fact about Taylor you didn't know... Most celebrities have tattoos, yet this starlet is scared of the needle. In 2019, Taylor debuted a massive back tattoo on the cover for her single You Need To Calm Down, but the shocking ink turned out to be fake (duh!).

She did reveal that if she were to ever get one (which is highly unlikely), it would be a tattoo of her lucky number, 13. "I don't think I could ever commit. I don't think I could ever commit to something permanent," she told Taste of Country.

21. Taylor's Idol is Shania Twain
Well, who doesn't love a bit of Shania, anyway? But T-Swift is completely obsessed with the country star and has openly spoken about the influence that Shania's had on her music. The adoration is completely mutual; Shania even told Entertainment Tonight that she admires Tay's honesty.

22. She's Feuded with Many Celebs

Indeed, Taylor Swift is one of the many celebrities that has caused controversy over the years. In fact, she's been famously involved in several celebrity feuds such as her fight with Katy Perry (but they've now made up), Kim Kardashian, Demi Lovato and Nicki Minaj.

23. Kim Kardashian (and Kanye) Made Her Move Country

In her interview with TIME Magazine, Taylor reflected on the "horrendous" moment in 2018 when Kim Kardashian and Kanye West tried to orchestrate a "frame job" against her. When Kanye released his song Famous that included an offensive lyric about Taylor, she insisted it wasn't approved by her.

Kim (Kanye's then wife) then released footage of Kanye's phone call with Taylor during which Tay appeared to approve the lyric.

Saying that she felt her "career was taken away," Taylor told TIME,

"You have a fully manufactured frame job, in an illegally recorded phone call, which Kim Kardashian edited and then put out to say to everyone that I was a liar," she added. "That took me down psychologically to a place I've never been before. I moved to a foreign country. I didn't leave a rental house for a year. I was afraid to get on phone calls. I pushed away most people in my life because I didn't trust anyone anymore. I went down really, really hard."

24. Two of her Videos are in the Top Viewed
That's right! Taylor has not one, but two clips that have made it into the most-viewed music videos of all time! Blank Space and Shake It Off are two of the singer's most popular music videos on YouTube, having been watched over three billion times each!

25. She's Still Tight With Her Childhood Friends
It says a lot about a celebrity when they still hang out with their day-one besties, and Taylor knows how to keep it real! She is still super close with her childhood friend Britany Maack, to whom she was her maid of honor in 2016.

26. Her Mom Wanted Her to Be an Equestrian
Growing up, Taylor loved horses and spent hours on the field riding them, mainly due to the fact that her mom shared the same passion. She spent the best part of her childhood riding competitively, until age 12 when she told her mom that she wasn't that into it anymore, and no longer wanted to pursue her hobby.

"That was kind of my mom's thing…" Taylor told Vogue. "…I just wanted to make music and do theater. So I've been a big disappointment."

"I've gotten over the bitterness, finally," Andrea said sarcastically.

27. Taylor's Not Afraid of Junk Food

Here's a fun fact about Taylor! Her secret craving is an all-American cheesecake! While Swifty maintains a balanced diet, she also indulges in some drive-through take-outs once in a while, too, with her go-to order being a cheeseburger, fries and a shake! If that's not BFF goals, I don't know what is!

28. She's Suffered from an Eating Disorder

Sadly, Taylor is one of the many celebrities who has had an eating disorder. Although the singer is now healthy and has overcome her struggles, that's not to say she hasn't fought a difficult battle in the past. Taylor has admittedly gone through an unhealthy cycle of avoiding food after feeling like she was constantly criticized for being too big or too thin.

In her documentary, Miss Americana, she said, "I thought that I was supposed to feel like I was going to pass out at the end of a show, or in the middle of it. Now I realize, no, if you eat food, have energy, get stronger, you can do all these shows and not feel (enervated)."

29. She Watches 'Friends' After Her Gigs

What better to unwind than with a bit of light comedy? Instead of partying the night away, Taylor revealed to GQ that she likes to go home and relax with a mini-marathon of Friends after performing to a large crowd. Watching your favorite TV show is certainly one way to calm down after the adrenaline rush of being onstage...

30. She Also Eats In Bed Between Shows
In between her hectic tour schedule, particularly the Eras
Tour, Taylor has admitted to eating her meals in bed for
recovery. She told TIME Magazine, "I do not leave my bed
except to get food and take it back to my bed and eat it
there. It's a dream scenario. I can barely speak because I've
been singing for three shows straight."

31. Taylor Has Three Furry Friends
Taylor is a major cat person, and has three fluffy friends of
her own. Her oldest cat is named Olivia Benson, after the
Law and Order: Special Victims Unit character, and her
second feline friend is called Meredith Grey, inspired by the
icon in Grey's Anatomy. In 2019, she rescued a new kitty and
named him Benjamin Button. #Cute!

32. Taylor Had a Listening Party With 89 Fans
Before the release of 1989, Swift invited 89 of her biggest
fans over to her house to listen to her album. Taylor put on a
show and even baked pumpkin chocolate-chip cookies for
her guests. Not to mention, she even had a dance party with
them, too! The special ordeal was verified by Swift blogger
Sammie Carter on her Tumblr account.

33. She Loves Connecting With Her Fans
Taylor once saw that #ShakeItOffJalene was trending on
Twitter and decided to act on it. The hashtag referred to a
four-year-old child who was battling with terminal brain
cancer and wished to dance to Shake It Off with the singer.
So, Taylor immediately jumped on FaceTime and fulfilled
this sweet girl's wish.

34. She Once Modeled For Abercrombie

Taylor definitely has that noughties Abercrombie & Fitch look, so it comes as no surprise that the model-esque singer once took a jab at a modeling career. In 2003, she posed in Abercrombie's 'Rising Stars' campaign, which gave her a good platform to get noticed in the industry.

35. Taylor Owns a Private Jet

Forget renting private planes, Taylor Swift now has her own airline – like many other big money makers. Instead of slumming it in first class, the Evermore singer has her own jet to fly her where and when she needs – a Dassault Falcon 900 private jet to be exact!

36. She's a Huge Disney Fan

This piece of trivia truly makes the singer relatable to all Disney nerds. Taylor never grew out of the Disney phase and is a huge fan up until this day (do you blame her?!).

37. She is One of the World's Richest Self-Made Women

In 2022, Taylor Swift ranked as the third "Richest Self-Made Woman Under 40" by Forbes. In 2023, she made another huge achievement, ranking at fourth place. Falling just behind Orpah Winfrey, Rihanna, and Kim Kardashian, with a net worth of $740 million, Swifty has clearly made her mark on the industry and achieved great success over the last decade.

38. Taylor Has Double-Jointed Elbows

During her interview with Vogue's 73 Questions, the star revealed that she has double-jointed elbows. Another talent that she can add to her ever-growing list!

39. She Has Her Social Media Comments Turned Off
To drown out the negativity and protect her own sanity,
Taylor Swift keeps the comments on her social profiles
turned off.

She told Elle, "One thing I do to lessen this weird insecurity
laser beam is to turn off comments. Yes, I keep comments
off on my posts. That way, I'm showing my friends and fans
updates on my life, but I'm training my brain to not need the
validation of someone telling me that I look [fire emojis]."

40. She Was the First to Write Her Own SNL Monologue
Seen as she co-writes all of her music, it's no shocker that
Taylor wanted to control her narrative while hosting SNL in
2009. Normally, a bunch of the team's in-house writers
prepare the monologues, but Swifty changed the game when
she wrote her own words for the iconic "My Monologue
Song".

41. Taylor Called Out the TV Show 'Ginny & Georgia'
Taylor Swift's dating history has always been the talk of the
town, with many ridiculing the amount of guys she's dated.
One TV show to make a mockery out of Tay's romantic life
was Ginny & Georgia, where the line, "What do you care? You
go through men faster than Taylor Swift," was used in a fight
scene between mother and daughter.

FACT 2

She framed a photo of the infamous Kanye West VMA
scandal for her apartment.
Taylor has a framed photo of the moment Kanye West
hijacked her acceptance speech during the 2009 VMAs in
the living room of her Nashville duplex, according to a
reporter at New York magazine who interviewed her there. It
hangs above a handwritten note that reads: Life is full of
little interruptions.

Blake Lively's daughter, James, is featured and credited on
Taylor's song "Gorgeous."
Taylor featured Blake's oldest daughter saying "gorgeous"
for the first line of "Gorgeous" on her album Reputation.
James receives her due credit in the album's booklet: "Baby
intro voice by James Reynolds."

She grew up on a Christmas tree farm.
Born in Reading, PA, Taylor spent the first 14 years of her life
living on a Christmas tree farm with her family, per People.
Plus, the house wasn't too shabby either. The six-bedroom
home sold for $700,000 in 2013, according to Zillow.

She learned to play guitar on a 12-string.
Despite being told her hands were too small, Taylor learned
to play a 12-string guitar before ever picking up a six-string.
Her mother told Entertainment Weekly, "She started playing
it four hours a day— six on the weekends. She would get
calluses on her fingers and they would crack and bleed, and
we would tape them up and she'd just keep on playing."

She is the youngest person to get a songwriting deal at Nashville's Sony/ATV Music Publishing.
At 14 years old, after turning down a deal with RCA Records because she wouldn't have the opportunity sing her own music, she signed with Sony/ATV Music Publishing in Nashville, according to Entertainment Weekly.

She's named after James Taylor.
Taylor's parents are big fans, and so named her after the musician, according to Vogue. Taylor got the chance to perform with her namesake at a benefit in 2011.

She has film and television credits on her resumé too.
You can look forward to seeing Taylor in the film adaptation of Cats which is set to begin filming this November. While you wait for its premiere, check out Taylor's performances in The Giver, New Girl, and CSI: Crime Scene Investigation.

She's the youngest Grammy winner for album of the year.
Taylor took home a trophy in 2010 for her album Fearless. At 20 years old, she is the youngest person to receive the honor.

She wrote and sang her hit "Our Song" for her ninth-grade talent show.
A hit single on her debut album, "Our Song" was originally written for a school performance and ended up making it onto her album Taylor Swift, per CMT News.

Her middle name is Alison.
While she's known as Swifty, T-Swizzle, Tay, and T.Swift, she's officially Taylor Alison Swift.

TIME magazine included Taylor in its 2017 Person of the Year edition.
Taylor was interviewed as a Silence Breaker for speaking out and testifying against the man she accused of grabbing her butt during a meet-and-greet in 2013. After he was fired from his job following her report of the incident, he sued her for defamation. She countersued for $1 and won. When asked what her fans should take away from her experience, Taylor answered, "My advice is that you not blame yourself and do not accept the blame others will try to place on you."

She only performed one show in 2017.
During her pre-Super Bowl set for DIRECTV Now Super Saturday Night, the singer announced it would be her only performance of the year. She told the crowd, "I have to be really honest with you about something: As far as I know, I'm doing one show in 2017. And as far as I know, this is that one show."

She has an app.
To get the latest updates on the singer's life Taylor Swift: The Swift Life promises users the ability to interact with each other and gives them access to photos and Taymoji stickers.

When she started out, her record label, Big Machine Label Group, had no furniture.
A young Taylor would sit on the floor of the start-up label and stuff envelops with her record to send to radio stations because recording with Big Machine meant creative control, per the Los Angeles Times. Now a major label, Big Machine represents talents including Florida Georgia Line, Thomas Rhett, and Sugarland.

She ditched the blonde locks for a hot sec.
For Sugarland's "Babe" music video, Taylor threw us for a loop and donned a red wig. But this wasn't the first time she sported the fiery look. Tay had red hair in her celeb-filled "Bad Blood" music video in 2014.

Reputation is the first album on which she uses a curse word.
In her song "I Did Something Bad," Taylor sings "If a man talks shit, then I owe him nothing."

Her album Speak Now was written by her and only her.
In response to critics who doubted the singer/songwriter had been writing her own music, Taylor wrote her third studio album on her own with the exception of one song she co-wrote with Martin Johnson, per TIME. Before this, she collaborated with co-writers on her songs.

Paparazzi determine whether or not she'll leave her house.
Proving she's just like us, Taylor is "perfectly happy staying in." She told TIME, "I try to evaluate whether I'm in the right emotional space to deal with that, and if I'm not, then I just stay in."

She's the reason GoFundMe increased its donation limit.
When Taylor donated $50,000 toward a fan's medical bills, the money had to be processed in four installments because of the site's donation cap. After this, GoFundMe upped the maximum donation limit to $50,000, according to People.

She wasn't really in England for work.
In an effort to keep her relationship with Joe Alwyn private, Taylor would tell people she was in England "for work," according to E!.

Her celebrity-studded Fourth of July party served as Ed Sheeran's first date with his fiancé.
Every year Instagram awaits photos from Taylor's Rhode Island Independence Day bash with bated breath. Ed Sheeran told People he'd invited an old friend, Cherry Seaborn, to Taylor's annual celebration in 2015, and the two are now engaged.

Kanye West blames T.Swift for his album getting such little radio airtime.
They're feuding, then they're not, then they are again. When Kanye's album Saint Pablo didn't get as much love on the radio as the rapper and designer would have liked, he blamed the very public dispute regarding whether Taylor approved of his referring to her as "that bitch" in his song "Famous." In an interview with Charlemagne tha God, Kanye said, "Really ever since the Taylor Swift moment, it just, it's never been the same."

She was a bridesmaid in her best friend Abigail's wedding.
Yes, the same Abigail she sings about in her song "Fifteen." Taylor's BFF got married last year and Taylor held Abigail's train before she took her first steps down the aisle, per Billboard.

13 is her lucky number.
The singer was born on December 13, and has incorporated the number in her music many times. Her fans have pinpointed the singer's deliberate uses of the number including a 13-second song intro or leaving the 13th track off of her latest album during early release to build anticipation.

She's a United States history buff.
In 2011, Taylor told Rolling Stone about her interest in reading about the early days of the United States, including books about the Founding Fathers and the Kennedy family.

She has a brother named Austin.
Austin Swift is an actor and he's two years younger than his sister.

She owns real estate across four states.
With three properties in New York alone, Taylor can call multiple states home. Her houses, estates, and apartments are estimated to be valued at $84 million total, according to property values estimated by Trulia for Business Insider.

She wouldn't allow her music to stream on Spotify.
In 2014, Taylor wrote an op-ed for The Wall Street Journal saying, "It's my opinion that music should not be free." However, in 2017 following record-breaking album sales, she finally allowed her albums to stream on the platform.

Her first job was debugging Christmas trees on her family's farm.
"We all had jobs," Taylor told Vogue, "Mine was picking the praying mantis pods off of the trees, collecting them so that the bugs wouldn't hatch inside people's houses."

Her legs were rumored to be insured for $40 million.

FACT 3

Taylor Swift Age

The multi-talented singer-songwriter, Taylor Alison Swift was born on December 13, 1989, in Reading, Pennsylvania. Taylor Swift's parents, Scott Kingsley Swift and Andrea Finlay supported her dreams since she was a little girl. She also has a younger brother, Austin Swift.

Interestingly enough, Taylor was reportedly named after James Taylor.

Taylor Swift Height

In addition to her bigger-than-life reputation as a musical artist, Taylor Swift is actually really tall. She stands at a whopping 5'11" and has always felt "freakishly tall."

Taylor First Worked in Musical Theater

At the young age of nine, Taylor Swift worked in musical theater. This allowed her to perform in the Berks Youth Theatre Academy productions four different times. It was a great experience for her that helped shape her stage presence.

This was also the time period when she had dreams of performing on Broadway. She remembers traveling to New York many times and standing in long lines to audition for various shows.

Her Inspiration was Shania Twain

Everyone had someone they look up to and admire. For Taylor Swift, it was none other than Shania Twain. When Swift heard Twain's music, she knew she wanted to make country music. It gave her a sense of wonder and enjoyment that she had never felt before in her life.

She was Taught How to Play Guitar by a Computer Repairman

At age twelve, Taylor took guitar lessons from a computer repairman, who also knew a thing or two about songwriting. This was the first step in her musical career.

Because of these lessons, Taylor wrote her first song, "Lucky You."

She Once Modeled for Abercrombie & Fitch

In 2003, she was part of their "Rising Stars" campaign. This was a great foot in the door for Taylor Swift.

Taylor is Multi-Talented

Most people already know about Taylor's musical chops and abilities to captivate an audience in a single note. But, did you know that she also plays several instruments including guitar, piano, ukelele, banjo, and electric guitar?

She has also been on several television shows and movies playing either herself like she did in the Hannah Montana Movie or playing a role as she did on the hit show CSI where she played Haley Jones.

Taylor also starred in the movie Valentine's Day and The Giver.

Taylor Swift Owns a Private Jet

Gone are the days of touring in a van for Taylor. Now she flies in her very own private jet. This purchase is said to be influenced by actor Jake Gyllenhall, which she made a few years after he flew her to London and back in 2010.

Taylor Swift Grew Up on a Christmas Tree Farm

Taylor Swift's father worked as a stockbroker, but they also owned a Christmas tree farm in Reading, Pennsylvania, where Taylor grew up from ages 5-10, with her brother, Austin. It makes sense why Christmas is her favorite holiday out of the whole year.

Her family later moved to the Nashville, Tennessee area so Taylor could be closer to the country music world. They lived in a lakehouse in Henderson, Tennessee.

Her Dad Owns Part of her Record Label

Her father, Scott Swift purchased 3% of the record label that signed Taylor Swift, Big Machine Records, in Nashville, Tennessee, at an estimated $120,000. It's believed that her dad also bought the first 100,000 records of her album day-of release to fudge the numbers on the billboard charts.

Her Favorite Food Is Cheesecake

When she is looking for a great snack after a long performance, she turns to the delicious treat of cheesecake. It is her favorite food.

She was the Youngest Country Music Artist to Write a #1 song

Taylor Swift was only 14 years old when she wrote "Our Song." She played the song at her 9th-grade talent show. The track was #1 on the charts. The music video was named Video Of The Year at the CMT Music Awards in 2008.

She Loves Anything and Everything Disney

Taylor has even described herself as obsessed with Disney cartoons. She was even the voice for one of the characters in The Lorax. This shows she is a wholesome young woman that enjoys things that are heartfelt and thoughtful.

Taylor Swift Boyfriends

Taylor Swift's dating history includes several famous actors and celebrities. This list includes actor, Jake Gyllenhaal, Jonas Brothers member, Joe Jonas, One Direction singer, Harry Styles, songwriter, John Mayer, and DJ Calvin Harris.

It's been said that "I Knew You Were Trouble" was written about Jake Gyllenhaal. So boys beware. If the relationship doesn't end well, she will probably write a breakup song about you.

Her current boyfriend at the time of this writing is an actor named, Joe Alwyn. She has been seeing him since 2017.

The AMA Recently Named her "Artist of the Decade"

This is quite an achievement for Taylor Swift, and it is one that means a great deal to her. It proves that she has staying power with her audience. Taylor keeps churning out hit after hit and there doesn't appear to be anything slowing her down.

Taylor Swift has Taken Home Many Awards for Her Talents

At the 2010 Grammy Awards, Taylor won Album of the Year for her second studio album Fearless. At 20 years old, this award made her the youngest artist in history to win this award.

In 2011, Billboard named Taylor Swift Woman of the year.

She also won her first BRIT award in 2015 for International Female Solo Artist.

The Number Thirteen Follows her Everywhere

Taylor Swift is very superstitious. The number 13 is her favorite number. She believes 13 is her lucky number. She ensures this number is on almost everything she owns. She even had a sticker of the number 13 stuck to the nose of her jet plane. She also writes 13 on her hand before each concert. Someone should inform her that tattoos are a thing.

Some of the reasons why Taylor claims it's a lucky number is because she was born on the 13th, she turned 13 years old on Friday the 13th. Taylor's first record achieved gold status in 13 weeks. She even goes as far as noticing her first #1 song had a 13-second introduction. If you ask me, this is a little crazy

Taylor Swift Albums

Throughout her career thus far, Taylor Swift has blown the music industry away with her phenomenal albums and songs. From her first album to her many other studio albums, Taylor has shown that she is not only a great singer-songwriter but a great performer as well.

Here is a list of her studio albums thus far:
Taylor Swift – 2006
Fearless – 2008
Speak Now – 2010
Red –2012
1989 – 2014
Reputation – 2017
Lover – 2020
Evermore – 2020

Taylor's third album, Speak Now was the first one to be written solely by her. This album landed at the number one spot on the U.S. Billboard 200 chart after its release.

She Once Sang at a Philadelphia 76ers game

When she was 11 years old, Taylor Swift sang "The Star-Spangled Banner" at a Philadelphia 76ers game.

It was also when she was 11 years old that she won a talent competition for singing Leann Rimes song, "Big Deal."

Taylor Broke a Country Music Record

She broke this country music record by selling more than $20 million hits, which was the most digital downloads of her songs than any other country artist.

Taylor Swift and Kanye West's Back and Forth

What some people call a feud between the two artists started in 2009 when Taylor was awarded the Best Female Video at the MTV Video Music Awards for her song "You Belong With Me." While giving her acceptance speech, West came on stage to tell her that Beyonce's video was actually the best.

Since this incident, the two have gone back and forth with many public whirlwind adventures, many of which often trending on social media platforms everywhere.

Top 10 Taylor Swift Songs of All Time

Although it is well known that Taylor Swift has many hit songs that have won many accolades over the years, there are a few of her songs that people will never forget and are often found singing along to.

Here are her top 10 songs of all time according to Rolling Stone:

"All Too Well" – 2021
"New Romantics" – 2014
"Mirrorball" – 2020
"Delicate" – 2017
"August" – 2020
"Long Live" – 2010
"Lover" – 2019
"Blank Space" – 2014
"Marjorie" – 2020 – which was written for her grandmother Marjorie Finlay who was an opera singer.
"Dear John" – 2010

While these are her top-rated songs, many people still are found singing the words to songs like "Love Story," "You Belong With Me," and her first single, "Tim McGraw."

Taylor Swift Net Worth

Taylor Swift's net worth in 2022, according to reports is estimated at $400 million.

QUIZ 1

1. What was Taylor's first album?
"Taylor Swift"
"Fearless"
"Speak Now"

2. How many songs did Taylor write or cowrite on her debut
album?
three songs
seven songs
every song

3. What's Taylor's middle name?
Jennifer
Alison
Hayden

4. What famous country singer is name-checked on Taylor's
first album's tracklist?
Dolly Parton
Faith Hill
Tim McGraw

4. Taylor lived on what kind of farm as a youngster?
dairy farm
Christmas tree farm
apple orchard

5. What is Taylor's second album?
"I Am Not OK"
"Speak Now"
"Fearless"

6. How many songs did Taylor take sole credit for writing on
her first album?
two
three
seven

7. How many songs did Taylor write alone on "Fearless?"
seven
four
two

8. What film has two Taylor-written songs on the
soundtrack?
"High School Musical"
"Camp Rock"
"Hannah Montana: The Movie"

9. What category did Taylor win when Kanye West
interrupted her MTV Video Music Award acceptance
speech?
Breakthrough Video
Video of the Year
Best Female Video

10. What's Taylor's lucky number?
7
13
2

11. Taylor was nominated for Best New Artist at the 2008
Grammys. Who won?
Taylor
Amy Winehouse
Paramore

12. Where was Taylor born?
Pennsylvania
Tennessee
Texas

13. How many Grammys did Taylor win in 2010?
two
four
one

14. How many songs did Taylor write (solo) on her third album, "Speak Now?"
nine
all of them
none of them

15. What show did Taylor appear on in 2009?
"How I Met Your Mother"
"Hannah Montana"
"CSI"

16. Swift named her fifth album "1989" because:
It was the year she was born.
It's her second favorite number.
It was the year her brother was born.

17. Swift says that "1989" is her first:
break up album
good album
pop album

18. Who was Taylor named for?
Zachary Taylor, 12th President of the United States
James Taylor
Elizabeth Taylor

19. What was Taylor's first No. 1 on the Billboard Hot 100 chart?
"Shake It Off"
"Trouble"
"We Are Never Ever Getting Back Together"

20. What service did Taylor remove her music from?
Spotify
Tidal
YouTube

21. What ensemble movie marked Taylor's big screen debut?
"Valentine's Day"
"He's Just Not That Into You"
"Love Actually"

22. What ensemble movie marked Taylor's big screen debut?
"Valentine's Day"
"He's Just Not That Into You"
"Love Actually"

23. What artist covered the entire "1989" album?
Ed Sheeran
Ryan Adams
Jack Antonoff

24. What is one Guinness World Record that Taylor holds?
Most Fans
Fastest Selling Single in Digital History
Most Hula Hooping While Singing

25. Taylor donated $50,000 to whom in 2014?
the Seattle Symphony
Hillary Clinton's Super PAC
the Humane Society

26. Taylor's brother is a graduate of what college?
Boston College
Julliard
University of Notre Dame

27. Taylor describes herself as:
a feminist
not a feminist
afraid of feminists

28. What does Taylor claim as her spirit animal?
a kitten
a fox
a hippo

29. What are Taylor's cat's names?
Olivia Benson and Meredith Grey
Olivia Pope and Dana Scully
Meredith Grey and Rachel Green

30. By 2016, how many Grammys has Taylor won?
eight
nine
ten

ANSWER 1

1. Released in 2006, Taylor released the album when she was just 17.

2. Like Mozart and Yo-Yo Ma before her, Taylor was an early musical prodigy.

3. Which explains my "TAS 4 LIFE" tattoo.

4. "Tim McGraw" was the first single from Swift.

5. Like Taylor would ever come from some suburban cul de sac.

7. "Fearless" came out in 2008.

8. Taylor took solo songwriting credit on three "Taylor Swift" songs.

9. Taylor's songwriting was getting bolder.

10. It's nice to imagine Taylor was so inspired by "HM: TM" that the songs just came pouring out.

11. And then we never heard another thing about Taylor again.

12. Taylor was born on the 13th of December, but she claims the number has been good luck in many ways for her..

13. It was Taylor's first Grammy nomination.

14. Austin Swift is Fightin' Irish.

`15. Taylor embraces equality for women and doesn't shy away from pointing out that misogyny is still rampant in our society.

16. Taylor says it's because they have to hide a lot, but one could also argue she's wily like one.

17. From "SVU" and "Grey's Anatomy," Taylor is down with female leads.

18. After three wins in 2016, Taylor's Grammy total fills both hands.

19. Country girl was born a northerner.

20. But who didn't win multiple Grammy's their 21st year? Yawn.

21. Taylor wrote every song herself on "Speak Now."

22. She played a DNA sample. Kidding, she played a teenager.

23. 1989 marked the first year of the Common Era of Taylor.

24. While she kept one foot firmly dangling in country waters before, "1989" marked her first foray into pure pop songwriting.

25. Sweet Baby James beget Sweet Baby Taylor.

26. The single from "Red" was a serious hit.

27. Unhappy with royalties paid to musicians, Taylor
removed her catalog from Spotify in 2014.

28. Taylor played Taylor Lautner's girlfriend in the film,
which must've been so confusing.

29. Ryan Adams is so prolific that he'll even record other
people's albums in his spare time.

30. She should really go for the hula hooping thing, though.

QUIZ 2

1. What is Taylor Swift's middle name?
Answer: Alison

2. Where was Taylor Swift born?
Answer: West Reading, Pennsylvania

3. What is Taylor Swift's mom's name?
Answer: Andrea

4. What is Taylor Swift's dad's name?
Answer: Scott

5. What is Taylor Swift's brother's name?
Answer: Austin

6. What was the song name of the track she wrote for Rihanna?
Answer: "This Is What You Came For"

7. What is Taylor Swift's birthday?
Answer: December 13, 1989

8. What was Taylor Swift's first single?
Answer: "Tim McGraw"

9. Which two Taylor Swift songs are allegedly about John Mayer?
Answer: "Dear John" and "Would've, Could've, Should've"

10. What was the name of the tour Taylor Swift had been planning for 2020?
Answer: Lover Fest

11. How many album covers feature Taylor Swift's super curly hair?
Answer: Three—her debut album, Fearless and Speak Now

12. Does Taylor Swift have any album covers in black and white?
Answer: Yes, two—reputation and folklore

13. Which album did Taylor Swift write by herself, without any co-writers?
Answer: Speak Now

14. What artist is Taylor Swift named after?
Answer: James Taylor

15. What is Taylor Swift's favorite number?
Answer: 13

16. What is at least one of Taylor Swift's cat's names?
Answer: Meredith Grey, Olivia Benson and Benjamin Button

17. How many albums does Taylor Swift have?
Answer: 10 albums

18. What type of farm did Taylor Swift grow up on?
Answer: A Christmas tree farm

19. Who is Taylor Swift's best friend from high school?
Answer: Abigail Anderson (now Abigail Anderson Berard)

20. What does "TV" stand for in reference to Taylor Swift's music?
Answer: "Taylor's Version" (AKA her re-recorded albums)

21. Who is "Back To December" rumored to be about?
Answer: Taylor Lautner

22. What were the listening parties called that Taylor Swift hosted for fans?
Answer: Secret Sessions

23. What is the order of Taylor Swift's albums from oldest to most recent?
Answer: Taylor Swift (Debut), Fearless, Speak Now, Red, 1989, reputation, Lover, folklore, evermore, Midnights

24. What song did Taylor Swift swap out early in The Eras Tour for "the 1" instead?
Answer: "Invisible String"

25. What classic book is referenced in "New Romantics"?
Answer: The Scarlet Letter by Nathaniel Hawthorne

26. What classic book is referenced in "This Is Why We Can't Have Nice Things"?
Answer: The Great Gatsby by F. Scott Fitzgerald

27. What famous couple is referenced in one of Taylor Swift's songs off of reputation?
Answer: Elizabeth Taylor and Richard Burton (in "...Ready For It?")

28. What Taylor Swift song includes the lyric: "November flush and your flannel cure"?
Answer: "champagne problems"

29. What Taylor Swift song features The Chicks?
Answer: "Soon You'll Get Better"

30. Which two actors did Taylor Swift feature in her All Too Well short film?
Answer: Sadie Sink and Dylan O'Brien

31. What is Taylor Swift's go-to drink order at the bar?
Answer: Vodka and Diet Coke

32. What color eyes does Taylor Swift mention in "Sparks Fly"?
Answer: Green

33. What exact time is referenced in "Last Kiss"?
Answer: 1:58

34. What is Taylor Swift's grandmother's full name?
Answer: Marjorie Finlay

35. What song did Taylor Swift cover in 2014 in the BBC Radio 1 Live Lounge?
Answer: "Riptide" by Vance Joy

36. What was Taylor Swift's songwriting pseudonym when working with then-boyfriend Calvin Harris?
Answer: Nils Sjoberg

37. What classic story-turned-Disney-movie is referenced in a song on the folklore album?
Answer: Peter Pan (the lyric "Peter losing Wendy" on "cardigan")

38. What "really cool or bizarre" fact did Taylor Swift share in her "73 Questions" Vogue video interview?
Answer: She has double-jointed elbows

39. What is Taylor Swift's longest song title?
Answer: "We Are Never Ever Getting Back Together"

40. List the years that each of Taylor Swift's 10 albums were released (in order).
Answer: 2006, 2008, 2010, 2012, 2014, 2017, 2019, 2020, 2020, 2022

41. What brand did Taylor Swift previously model for?
Answer: Abercrombie

42. What was the first surprise song to be repeated on The Eras Tour?
Answer: "Clean"

43. What's the name of Taylor Swift's previous violin player who's recently been playing with Kelsea Ballerini?
Answer: Caitlin Evanson

44. What flavor are Taylor Swift's famous cookies?
Answer: Chai Tea

45. What are all of the track fives from every Taylor Swift album?
Answer: "Cold As You," "White Horse," "Dear John," "All Too Well," "All You Had To Do Was Stay," "Delicate," "The Archer," "my tears ricochet," "tolerate it" and "You're On Your Own, Kid"

46. What two parks are mentioned in two of Taylor Swift's songs?
Answer: Centennial Park and the High Line

47. Taylor Swift had a cameo in what episode of New Girl?
Answer: The season 2 finale, Cece and Shivrang's wedding day

48. Which two Taylor Swift songs reference a "tightrope"?
Answer: "mirrorball" and "Innocent"

49. Which two Taylor Swift songs reference Taylor's dad interacting with her love interest?
Answer: "Last Kiss" and "All Too Well (10 Minute Version) (Taylor's Version)"

50. Name as many Taylor Swift songs as you can that have a number in their title.
Answer: "the 1," "22," "Fifteen," "The Lucky One" and "Two Is Better Than One"

QUIZ 3

What year was Taylor born?
She was born in 1989.

What is Taylor Swift's lucky number?
Thirteen is her favorite number.

Taylor won her first Grammy award for which song?
She won her first Grammy for the song White Horse.

Where was Taylor discovered?
Taylor was discovered at the Bluebird Cafe.

What was the title of Taylor's first album?
Taylor Swift was the name of her self-titled album.

What is Taylor Swift's middle name?
Her middle name is Alison.

How many Grammys did Taylor win in 2010?
She won four Grammy awards.

When did Taylor release her first album?
October 2006.

What famous rapper interrupted Taylor Swift's speech at the 2009 VMA's?
Kanye West.

How tall is Taylor Swift?
5 feet 10 inches.

What is the name of Taylor's childhood best friend?
Abigail Anderson.

What song earned Taylor a "Best Lyrics" award at the 2015
iHeartRadio Music Awards?
"Blank Space".

What record label did Taylor Swift first sign with?
Big Machine Records.

Who was Taylor named for?
James Taylor.

What is the name of Taylor's brother?
Austin.

Who did Taylor write "We Are Never Ever Getting Back
Together" about?
Jake Gyllenhaal.

What service did Taylor remove her music from?
Spotify.

In what song does Taylor sing: "Cause the players gonna
play, play, play, play, play"?
"Shake It Off".

Who did Taylor write "I Knew You Were Trouble" about?
Harry Styles.

When is Taylor's birthday?
Dec. 13, 1989.

What show did Taylor appear on in 2009?
CSI.

What are Taylor's cat's names?
Olivia Benson and Meredith Grey.

Where did Taylor move at the age of 14?
Nashville, Tennessee.

Taylor is the godmother of which celebrity's kid?
Jaime King.

In what song does Taylor sing: "He's got a one-hand feel on the steering wheel, the other on my heart"?
"Our Song"

Who taught Taylor how to play the guitar?
A repairman.

What artist covered the entire "1989" album?
Ryan Adams.

Taylor donated $50,000 to whom in 2014?
The Seattle Symphony.

Where was Taylor born?
Pennsylvania.

How many singles were released from Taylor's first album?
Five singles.

How many songs did Taylor write or co-write on her debut album?
Every song.

What is Taylor's second album?
Fearless.

What are the names of Taylor's parents?
Scott and Andrea Swift.

What song did Taylor write for her high school talent show?
Our Song.

What film has two Taylor-written songs on the soundtrack?
"Hannah Montana: The Movie".

How many songs did Taylor write alone on "Fearless?"
Seven.

Taylor was nominated for Best New Artist at the 2008
Grammys. Who won?
Amy Winehouse.

In what song does Taylor sing: "I guess you didn't care, and I
guess I liked that"?
"I Knew You Were Trouble".

In what song does Taylor sing: "She wears high heels, I wear
sneakers..."?
"You Belong with Me".

Taylor's first broadcast performance of "Tim McGraw" was
on what show?
Good Morning America.

Where did Taylor spend her early years?
A Pennsylvania Christmas tree farm.

Taylor Swift met actor Taylor Lautner on the set of what movie?
Valentine's Day.

What is Taylor Swift's favorite color?
Purple.

Which of Taylor's songs earned her a Guinness World Record for fastest selling single in digital history?
"We Are Never Ever Getting Back Together".

Taylor was the spokesperson for what NHL team?
Nashville Predators.

What was the lead single on Taylor Swift's debut album?
"Tim McGraw".

Taylor was the first country music artist to win an MTV Video Music Award when her song "You Belong with Me" was named Best Female Video in what year?
2009.

How many songs did Taylor write (solo) on her third album, "Speak Now?"
All of them.

Which singer collaborated with Swift on the single The Last Time?
Gary Lightbody.

Taylor's brother is a graduate of what college?
Notre Dame.

Taylor likes putting hidden messages in the lyric books of her albums. For which song was this the hidden message? 'You Thought I Would Forget'?
Better Than Revenge.

What was the name of Swift's her fourth album, released in 2012, which sold over one million copies in its first week of US release?
Evermore.

QUOTES

1. "I'm the type of person, I have to study to get an A on the test."

2. "I'd like to think you don't stop being creative once you get happy. My ultimate goal is to end up being happy. Most of the time."

3. "I think songwriting is the ultimate form of being able to make anything that happens in your life productive."

4. "Even if you're happy with the life you've chosen, you're still curious about the other options."

5. "My parents taught me never to judge others based on whom they love, what color their skin is, or their religion."

6. "Nashville is my home, and the reason why I get to do what I love."

7. "When you're singing you can hear the echo of people in the audience singing every single word with you, and that was that big dream that I had for myself. It's happening."

8. "I think who you are in school really sticks with you. I don't ever feel like the cool kid at the party, ever. It's like, 'Smile and be nice to everybody, because you were not invited to be here.'"

9. "Factoring in millions of people when I'm writing a song is not a good idea. I don't ever do it."

10. "I think the first thing you should know is that nobody in country music 'made it' the same way. It's all different. There's no blueprint for success, and sometimes you just have to work at it."

11. "When I get on a roll with something, it's really hard for me to put it down unfinished."

12. "If I'm gonna write songs about my exes, they can write songs about me. That's how it works."

13. "It's pretty intense writing about my own life, my own struggles."

14. "I think that you can love people without it being the great love."

15. "Getting a great idea with song writing is a lot like love. You don't know why this one is different, but it is. You don't know why this one is better, but it is. It sticks in your head, and you can't stop thinking about it."

16. "You can be obsessed with the bad things people say and the good things; either way, you're obsessed with yourself, and I'm not—you can become unhinged so easily."

17. "Anything you put your mind to and add your imagination into can make your life a lot better and a lot more fun."

18. "I think, as far as branching out with acting, it would take something really right on the mark to distract me from music, because music is everything to me."

19. "I have so many indie bands on my iPod. What I don't really understand is the attitude that if a band is unknown, they're good, and if they get fans, then you move on to the next band."

20. "Part of me feels you can't say you were truly in love if it didn't last. If I end up getting married and having kids, that's when I'll know it's real—because it lasted."

21. "I put out one album one week, and I'm already worried about the next one. I feel a lot of emotion throughout the course of a day. But not to the point where you need to be worried about me."

22. "Most of my songs have names of people I've met or are dear to me. There are people who have privacy issues and about people knowing about their private life. But for me, I like to include few special names and few details about them to make the song very special to me."

23. "When I'm 40 and nobody wants to see me in a sparkly dress anymore, I'll be like: 'Cool, I'll just go in the studio and write songs for kids.'"

24. "I think I first realized I wanted to be in country music and be an artist when I was 10. And I started dragging my parents to festivals, and fairs, and karaoke contests, and I did that for about a year before I came to Nashville for the first time. I was 11 and I had this demo CD of me singing Dixie Chicks and Leanne Rimes songs."

25. "I remember auditioning for record labels and having them tell me, 'Well, the country-radio demographic is the thirty-five-year-old female housewife. Give us a song that relates to the thirty-five-year-old female, and we'll talk.'"

26. "There's so much about Dolly Parton that every female artist should look to, whether it's reading her quotes or reading her interviews or going to one of her live shows. She's been such an amazing example to every female songwriter out there."

27. "Every single one of us has a few months here or there that feel like dark months."

28. "It's kind of exhilarating, walking through a crazy, insane mob. The most miraculous process is watching a song go from a tiny idea in the middle of the night to something that 55,000 people are singing back to you."

29. "My experience with songwriting is usually so confessional, it's so drawn from my own life and my own stories."

30. "All of my walls are covered with framed pictures of my friends."

31. "I have this fear of falling in front of large groups of people. That's why I tend not to wear heels."

32. "I base a lot of decisions on my gut, and going with an independent label was a good one."

33. "When I go to a restaurant, yeah, I know that a line is probably going to form in front of the table, but didn't I always wish for that? Yeah, I did."

34. "No matter what happens in life, be good to people. Being good to people is a wonderful legacy to leave behind."

35. "I love it when people say things to me in public and want to meet me, because I want to meet them! Early on, my manager told me, 'If you want to sell 500,000 records, then go out there and meet 500,000 people.'"

36. "You get to a point where it's like you can't really do anything right, and people will pick on you for whatever decisions you make, so I just try and take no notice and get on with my music."

37. "When I listen to a song, I don't say, 'Oh my gosh, that vocal line she sang was the best thing I ever heard.' I'm thinking, 'That lyric just moves me. That lyric just said what I feel better than I could say it myself.'"

38. "I'm a songwriter. Everything affects me."

39. "When I was a teenager, my biggest lessons came from Kenny Chesney, Tim McGraw, George Strait, Rascal Flatts and Brad Paisley. I learned so much from opening up for those artists, and it also taught me how to treat your opening acts and make them feel like they're part of a family, not just a tour."

40. "As your career grows, the list of things that makes you happy should not become smaller, it should become bigger."

41. "One of my big goals as a human being is to continue to write what's really happening to me, even if it's a tough pill to swallow for people around me... I do fear that if I ever were to have someone in my life who mattered, I would second-guess every one of my lyrics."

42. "I think I have a big fear of things spiraling out of control. Out of control and dangerous and reckless and thoughtless scares me, because people get hurt."

43. "When I'm in management meetings when we're deciding my future, those decisions are left up to me. I'm the one who has to go out and fulfill all these obligations, so I should be able to choose which ones I do or not. That's the part of my life where I feel most in control."

44. "I try to read as much as I can. I try to read an informative article every day. I try to stay read up on our world issues."

45. "I don't know how to have a normal relationship because I try to act normal and love from a normal place and live a normal life, but there is sort of an abnormal magnifying glass, like telescope lens, on everything that happens."

46. "I think the perfection of love is that it's not perfect."

47. "My audience has really become a very diverse group of people. It's not just 15-year-old girls. That's kind of what allows me to write from all the different places I want to write from."

48. "There's a lot of pressure putting an album out all over the world and hoping people everywhere like it."

49. "One element of Madonna's career that really takes center stage is how many times she's reinvented herself. It's easier to stay in one look, one comfort zone, one musical style. It's inspiring to see someone whose only predictable quality is being unpredictable."

50. "When we're falling in love or out of it, that's when we most need a song that says how we feel. Yeah, I write a lot of songs about boys. And I'm very happy to do that."

www.ingramcontent.com/pod-product-compliance
Lightning Source LLC
Chambersburg PA
CBHW051701250726
48653CB00007B/2785